A BOOK
OF
HOURS

Eus in adiutorium
meum intende
Domine ad ad
niuandum me festi

HENRI NOUWEN

A BOOK OF hOURS

Compiled by
ROBERT WALDRON

Seabury Books

Unless otherwise stated the Scripture quotations in this
publication are taken from the New Jerusalem Bible,
published and copyright © 1985 by Darton, Longman and Todd
Ltd and Doubleday, a division of Bantam Doubleday Dell
Publishing Group Inc.

Library of Congress Cataloging-in-Publication Data

A catalog record of this book is available from the
Library of Congress.

ISBN-13: 978-1-59627-112-8 (hardcover)

First published in Great Britain in 2009 by
Darton, Longman and Todd Ltd
1 Spencer Court, 140–142 Wandsworth High Street,
London SW18 4JJ

First published in the United States in 2009 by Seabury Books
445 Fifth Avenue, New York, New York 10016

www.seaburybooks.com

Designed and produced by Sandie Boccacci
Printed and bound in Great Britain by
Scotprint, Haddington, East Lothian

An imprint of Church Publishing Incorporated

5 4 3 2 1

Contents

Abbreviations

The quotations are from the following books by Henri Nouwen:

A:	*Adam*
CDC:	*Can You Drink the Cup?*
CR:	*Clowning in Rome*
G:	*The Genesee Diary*
HN:	*Here and Now*
I:	*Intimacy*
IVL:	*The Inner Voice of Love*
L:	*Lifesigns / Compassion*
LB:	*The Life of the Beloved*
MATN:	*Making All Things New*
PS:	*The Return of the Prodigal Son*
RO:	*Reaching Out*
SD:	*Spiritual Direction*
SJ:	*Sabbatical Journey*
SJs:	*Spiritual Journals*
SWC:	*The Selfless Way of Christ*
WBH:	*With Burning Hearts*
WH:	*The Way of the Heart*
WOH:	*With Open Hands*

Introduction:
Attending the Hours

In England, around the year 1240, William de Brailes of Oxford produced the first Book of Hours to have survived. He was not only a scribe but also a gifted illuminator. During the time before the printing press, the Book of Hours was hand-written and hand-painted on vellum made from the skins of sheep; it was written in Latin, *in imitatio* of the liturgical hours enclosed monks and nuns followed during their day, primarily centered on the recitation or chanting of the Psalms. The Book of Hours (in England called a Primer) also included 'The Little Office of the Blessed Virgin,' 'The Office for the Dead' (including seven Penitential Psalms), and 'The Litany of Saints.'[1]

The monastic day entailed seven canonical hours: Vigils, Matins with Lauds, Prime, Terce, Sext, None, and Vespers with Compline. The major hours of Vigils, Lauds, None, Vespers, and Compline were chanted communally; the minor day (small) hours of Matins, Prime, Terce, and Sext were also sung, but in today's Cistercian monasteries they are prayed privately. Thomas Merton writes, 'The Canonical Office is the total of psalms, hymns, lessons, antiphons, responsories, etc., officially instituted by the Church and imposed as a matter of obligation, to be recited daily by all monks and other religious under solemn vows as well as by the clerics in major orders.'[2]

Most Books of Hours were made for literate, aristocratic women, and they were highly treasured not only as prayer books but also as works of art, for they were often lavishly adorned with jewel-like paintings of scenes from the Bible or the lives of the saints; in England, scenes from the life of Thomas Becket were popular, particularly renditions of his martyrdom at the altar of Canterbury.

Before long, owning a beautifully scripted and illustrated Book of Hours became a status symbol. After the Black Death, wealthy English lay people were purchasing the Book of Hours, now produced in large numbers in stationers' shops in the Netherlands and France.

With the appearance of the printing press in the

late fifteenth century, the Book of Hours became a more popular form of devotion among the literate than the Psalter. Not only aristocrats but also plebeians had access to the Book of Hours, correlating their hours of worship with the holy prayer life of monks and nuns.

The Book of Hours was practical, its smallness easily fitting into a pocket or hidden in one's dress so that a person carried her 'cell' wherever she went. By 1530, the Book of Hours moved towards the vernacular, and the more English that was included within its pages, the more coveted it became. Even when England broke with Rome, the Book of Hours remained a devotional favorite, except that any references to the Pope or Saint Thomas Becket had to be obliterated. In fact, between 1558 and 1599, no Catholic Book of Hours was produced in England.

We are now in the twenty-first century, and I am encouraged by the increasing interest in *lectio divina*, primarily the result of Thomas Merton's writings as well as those of Kathleen Norris and Henri Nouwen. Lay people are again interested in prayer books like the Book of Hours, and the attraction is similar to the one it held in the Middle Ages. It is a small book, and if followed faithfully, it helps structure our day with prayer; thus, we not only sanctify our relationship with God, but we sanctify the minutes and hours of our day. We do not have an infinite amount of time on earth; therefore, it is our responsibility to ensure that our time is lived to the full, and we accomplish this best when we include in our life time for prayer, which is time for God.

From the time of Saint Benedict, cloistered monks and nuns lived a life of *ora et labora* (prayer and work). When the bell tolled, everyone stopped what he was doing to make his way to the sanctuary to pray. People offered their attention to sacred texts, particularly the Psalter, one hundred and fifty psalms, prayed and sung within the space of a week. I prefer, however, not to view a monk's day as a duality: divided into work *and* prayer. Prayer is also work (*opus dei*): it demands our complete attention; in fact, it requires an exquisite attention, the kind that allows for the disappearance of the ego, for in true prayer there occurs a self-forgetting so that God assumes the place of ego: a spiritual movement from I to Thou.

Each liturgical hour is a window. When one first gazes upon the window of a sacred text, one likely sees a reflection of the self. The window of the eye is cleansed by its attention upon the text, so that eye and text merge, permitting one to see beyond the I to God. But the possibilities of one's seeing (reading) depend upon the quality of one's *attending* the Hours. *Attending* comes from the French word *Attente*, the very word used by Simone Weil in her famous definition of prayer: 'Absolutely unmixed attention is prayer.' It also means 'waiting'; consequently, the translation of the title of her most famous book, *Attente de Dieu*, is *Waiting for God*, which has also been translated into English as *Waiting on God*. Waiting is an exquisitely attentive time fraught with expectancy. Therefore, when we attend to a sacred text, we are at our most attentive.

My dictionary offers these meanings for attend: to be present; to pay attention, heed; and to be ready to serve, wait. Thus I have chosen as the title of this introduction *Attending the Hours*. Although I am a great admirer of Eamon Duffy's wonderful, scholarly book, *Marking the Hours: English People and Their Prayers 1240–1570,* I do not think the true purpose of a Book of Hours is to mark them but rather to *attend* to them.

Following the still-honored *Horae Canonicae* of modern monastic orders throughout the world, I have composed a Book of Hours based upon the writings of Henri Nouwen, one of the greatest spiritual teachers of our time. His prose is suffused with references to the Bible and to the lives of saints. His writing is as transparent as a window with nothing to obscure our view of ourselves or of God. Henri Nouwen's books serve as *lectio divina* for thousands if not millions of people. He deeply understood the Christian call to prayer,

> We are called to be contemplatives, that is *see-ers*, men and women who are called to see the coming of God. The day of the Lord is indeed always coming. It is not a coming which will occur in some distant future, but a coming here and now among us. The Lord's coming is an ongoing event around us, between us, and within us. To become a contemplative,

therefore, means to throw off – or better, to peel off – the blindfolds that prevent us from seeing his coming in the midst of our world.[3]

In other words, Nouwen is calling on us to see, to attend to the hours of our day, for if we are truly attentive we will find God within and among us.

Henri Nouwen: A Book of Hours is organized into four weeks, a month of holy prayer. The Epilogue contains my essay, *Henri Nouwen's Theology of the Home as Love*.

I have arranged this book around the major hours followed by Thomas Merton's order, the Trappists, also known as Cistercians. They communally begin their day at Vigils at 3:00 a.m. and end it with Compline at 7:30 p.m. At the end of the day, the whole community sings in darkness the hymn *Salve Regina*, with a candle before an icon or stained glass window of the Virgin Mary.

I have also added the *Angelus* to the day's prayer; it is a prayer in honor of the Incarnation, commemorating the angel Gabriel's annunciation to the Blessed Virgin. Its opening words are, '*Angelus Domini nuntisvit Mariae*' ('the Angel of the Lord declared unto Mary.') To be read after the singing of the *Salve Regina* (the singing of this Marian hymn began in Cistercian monasteries in the thirteenth century) is a 'Bible Before Bed' passage for a final meditation. Thus, we honor with attentive holiness the hours of our day, from the moment we awaken to the moment we go to bed.

I hope that *Henri Nouwen: A Book of Hours* will help lead you into a deeper, more loving and attentive relationship with God.

Endnotes

1. Eamon Duffy, *Marking the Hours: English People and Their Prayers 1240–1570* (New Haven: Yale University Press, 2006).
2. Thomas Merton, *The Waters of Siloe* (New York: Harcourt, Brace and Company, 1949), p. 366.
3. Henri Nouwen, *The Road to Peace: Writings on Peace and Justice*, ed. John Dear (Orbis Books: New York, 1998), pp. 196–7.

WEEK ONE

SUNDAY

Vigils (early morning)

My reading about the spirituality of the desert
has made me aware of the importance of
'nepsis.' Nepsis means mental sobriety, spiritual
attention directed to God, watchfulness in
keeping the bad thoughts away, and creating
free space for prayer. While working with the
rocks I repeated a few times '*fuge, tace, et quiesce*'
('live in solitude, silence and inner peace'), but
only God knows how far I am, not only from
this reality but even from this desire. (G, p. 31)

Lauds (morning)

The more I spoke of the (Rembrandt's)
Prodigal Son, the more I came to see it as, somehow, my personal painting, the painting that
contained not only the heart of the story that
God wants to tell me, but also the heart of the

story that I want to tell to God, and God's people. All of the Gospel is there. All of my life is there. All of the lives of my friends is there. The painting has become a mysterious window through which I can step into the Kingdom of God. (PS, p. 15)

Angelus
The angel of the Lord brought tidings to Mary
And she conceived of the Holy Spirit.

Hail, Mary full of grace, the Lord is with thee: Blessed art thou among women, and blessed is The fruit of thy womb, Jesus. Holy Mary, Mother of God, pray for us sinners, now and at the hour of our death. Amen.

Behold the handmaid of the Lord:
Be it done unto me according to your word.

Hail, Mary …

And the Word was made flesh:

And dwelt among us.
Hail, Mary …

Pray for us, O holy Mother of God:
That we may be made worthy of the promises
of Christ.

We beseech thee, O Lord, to pour thy grace into
our hearts, that as we have known the incarnation of thy Son Jesus Christ by the message of
an angel, so by his cross and passion we may be
brought to the glory of his resurrection, through
the same Christ our Lord.

None (afternoon)

The spiritual life is not life before, after, or
beyond our everyday existence. No, the
spiritual life can only be real when it is lived in
the midst of the pains and joys of the here and
now. Therefore we need to begin with a care-
ful look at the way we think, speak, feel, and act
from hour to hour, day to day, week to week,

and year to year, in order to become more fully aware of our hunger for the spirit. As long as we have only a vague inner feeling of discontent with our present way of living, and only an indefinite desire for 'things spiritual,' our lives will continue to stagnate in a generalized melancholy. (MATN, p. 21)

Vespers (dusk)

Conversion is certainly not something you can bring about yourself. It is not a question of will-power. You have to trust the inner voice that shows the way. You know that inner voice. You turn to it often. But after you have heard with clarity what you are asked to do, you start raising questions, fabricating objections, and seeking everyone else's opinion. Thus you become entangled in countless often contradictory thoughts, feelings, and ideas and lose touch with God in you. And you end up dependent on all the people you have gathered around you. (IVL, p. 61)

Compline (evening)

When Jesus says: 'Make your home in me as I make mine in you,' he offers us an intimate place that we can truly call 'home.' Home is that place or space where we do not have to be afraid but can let go of our defenses and be free, free from worries, free from tensions, free from pressures. Home is where we can laugh and cry, embrace and dance, sleep long and dream quietly, eat, read, play, watch the fire, listen to music, and be with a friend. Home is where we can rest and be healed. (L, p. 27)

Salve Regina

Hail, holy Queen, Mother of mercy,
Our life, our sweetness and our hope.
To thee do we cry,
Poor banished children of Eve,
To thee do we send up our sighs,
Mourning and weeping
In this valley of tears.
Turn then, most gracious Advocate,

Thine eyes of mercy toward us,
And after this our exile,
Show unto us the blessed fruit
Of thy womb, Jesus.
O clement, O loving,
O sweet Virgin Mary!
Pray for us, O Holy Mother of God,
That we may be made worthy
Of the promises of Christ.
Amen.

Bible Before Bed

Listen, my children, to a father's instruction;
pay attention, and learn what understanding is.
What I am offering you is sound doctrine,
do not forsake my teaching.
I too was once a child with a father,
in my mother's eyes a tender child, unique.
This was what he used to teach me,
'Let your heart treasure what I have to say,
keep my principles and you will live.'

(Proverbs 4:1–4)

MONDAY

Vigils

Jesus, the only son of the Father, 'emptied himself and being as we are, he was humbler yet, even to accepting death, death on a cross. But God raised him high, and gave him the name which is above all other names (Philippians 2:7–9). Only through ultimate sameness was Jesus given his unique name. When St Paul calls us to have the mind of Jesus Christ, he invites us to that same humility through which we can become brothers of the Lord and sons of the heavenly Father. (G, p. 67)

Lauds

For most of my life I have struggled to find God, to know God, to love God. I have tried hard to follow the guidelines of the spiritual life – pray always, work for others, read the

Scriptures – and to avoid the many temptations to dissipate myself. I have failed many times but always tried again, even when I was close to despair … It might sound strange, but God wants to find me as much as, if not more than, I want to find God. (PS, p. 106)

Angelus
The Angel of the Lord brought tidings to Mary …

None
Jesus' response to our worry-filled lives is quite different. He asks us to shift the point of gravity, to relocate the center of our attention, to change our priorities. Jesus wants us to move from the 'many things' to the 'one necessary thing'. It is important for us to realize that Jesus in no way wants us to leave our many-faceted world. Rather, he wants us to live in it, but firmly rooted in the center of all things … He speaks about a change of heart. This change of

heart makes everything different, even while everything appears to remain the same. This is the meaning of 'Set you hearts on his kingdom first ... and all these other things will be given you as well.' (MATN, p. 42)

Vespers

Look at Rembrandt and van Gogh. They trusted their vocations and did not allow anyone to lead them astray. With true Dutch stubbornness, they followed their vocations from the moment they recognized them. They didn't bend over backward to please their friends or enemies. Both ended their lives in poverty, but both left humanity with gifts that could heal the minds and hearts of many generations of people. Think of these two men and trust that you too have a unique vocation that is worth claiming and living out faithfully. (IVL, p. 33)

Compline

A fruitful life is first of all lived in vulnerability.

As long as we remain afraid of each other we arm ourselves and live defensive lives. No fruits can come forth from such lives. They lead to walls, arms, and to the most sophisticated inventions, such as Trident submarines and cruise missiles, but they do not bear fruit. Only when we dare to lay down our protective shields and trust each other enough to confess our shared weakness and need can we live a fruitful life together. (L, p. 66)

Salve Regina
Hail, holy Queen, Mother of mercy …

Bible Before Bed
My child, pay attention to what I am telling
    you,
listen carefully to my words;
do not let them out of your sight,
keep them deep in your heart.
For they are life to those who find them
and health to all humanity. (Proverbs 4:20–3)

TUESDAY

Vigils

Now I know that it is not I who pray but the Spirit of God who prays in me. Indeed, when God's glory dwells in me, there is nothing too far away, nothing too painful, nothing too strange or too familiar that it cannot contain and renew by its touch. Every time I recognize the glory of God in me and give it space to manifest itself to me, all that is human can be brought there and nothing will be the same again. (G, p. 75)

Lauds

(Describing Rembrandt's *The Return of the Prodigal Son*)

In Latin, to bless is *benedicere*, which means literally: saying good things. The Father wants to say, more with his touch than with his voice, good things of his children. He has no desire to punish them. They have already been punished excessively by their own inner or outer waywardness. The Father wants simply to let them know that the love they have searched for in such distorted ways, has been, is and always will be there for them. The Father wants to say, more with his hands than with his mouth: 'You are my Beloved, on you my favor rests.' He is the shepherd, 'feeding his flock, gathering lambs in his arms, holding them against his breast.' (PS, p. 96)

Angelus
The Angel of the Lord brought tidings to Mary ...

None
This eternal community of love is the center and source of Jesus' spiritual life, a life of uninterrupted attentiveness to the Father in the Spirit of Love. It is from this life that Jesus'

ministry grows. His eating and fasting, his praying and acting, his traveling and resting, his preaching and teaching, his exorcising and healing, were all done in this Spirit of love. We will never understand the full meaning of Jesus' richly varied ministry unless we see how the many things are rooted in the one thing: listening to the Father in the intimacy of perfect love. (MATN, pp. 49–50)

Vespers

As you come to realize that God is beckoning you to a greater hiddenness, do not be afraid of that invitation. Over the years you have allowed the voices that call you to action and great visibility to dominate your life. You still think, even against your own best intuitions, that you need to do things and be seen in order to follow your vocation. But you are now discovering that God's voice is saying, 'Stay home, and trust that your life will be fruitful even when hidden.' (IVL, p. 89)

Compline

When we are no longer dominated by fear and have experienced the first love of God, we no longer need to know from moment to moment what is going to happen. We can trust that good things will happen if we remain rooted in that love. All true education, formation, and healing are ways to let the fruits of love grow and develop to full maturity. All ministry is caring attentiveness to vulnerable lives, and a grateful receiving of the variety of fruits by which they manifest their beauty. (L, p. 72)

Salve Regina

Hail, holy Queen, Mother of mercy …

Bible Before Bed

Listen you deaf!
Look and see, you blind!
Who so blind as my servant
So deaf as the messenger I send?

(Who so blind as the friend I have taken to
   myself,
So deaf as Yahweh's servant?)
You have seen many things,
But not observed them;
Your ears are open but you do not hear.

(Isaiah 42:18–20)

WEDNESDAY

Vigils
When I walked out I was overwhelmed by the beauty of the landscape unfolding itself before my eyes, bright colors of the trees. The yellow of the hickory trees, the different shades of red from the maples and oaks, the green of the willows – together they formed a fantastic spectacle. The sky was full of mysterious cloud formations, and just as I walked down to the guesthouse, the sun's rays burst through the clouds and covered the land with their light, making the cornfields look like a golden tapestry … I can only say with the psalmists: 'The hills are girded with joy, they shout for joy, yes, they sing.' (G, p. 157)

Lauds
One of the greatest challenges of the spiritual

life is to receive God's forgiveness. There is something in us humans that keeps us clinging to our sins and prevents us from letting God erase our past and offer us a completely new beginning. Sometimes it even seems as though I want to prove to God that my darkness is too great to overcome. While God wants to restore me to the full dignity of sonship, I keep insisting that I will settle for being a hired servant. Do I truly want to be so totally forgiven that a completely new way of living becomes possible? Do I want … to surrender myself so absolutely to God's love that a new person can emerge? (PS, p. 53)

Angelus
The Angel of the Lord brought tidings to Mary …

None
Without solitude it is virtually impossible to live a spiritual life. Solitude begins with a time

and place for God, and him alone. If we really believe not only that God exists but also that he is actively present in our lives – healing, teaching, and guiding – we need to set aside a time and space to give him our undivided attention. Jesus says, 'Go to your private room and, when you have shut your door, pray to your Father who is in that secret place' (Matthew 6:6). (MATN, p. 69)

Vespers

There is within you a lamb and a lion. Spiritual maturity is the ability to let lamb and lion lie down together. Your lion is your adult, aggressive self. It is your initiative-taking and decision-making self. But there is also your fearful, vulnerable lamb, the part of you that needs affection, support, affirmation and nurturing ...

The art of spiritual living is to fully claim both your lion and your lamb. Then you can act assertively without denying your own needs. And you can ask for affection and care without betraying your talent to offer leadership. (IVL, p. 78)

Compline

When we enter the household of God, we come to realize that the fragmentation of humanity and its agony grow from the false supposition that all human beings have to fight for their right to be appreciated and loved. In the house of God's love we come to see with new eyes and hear with new ears and thus recognize that all people, whatever their race, religion, sex, wealth, intelligence, or background, belong to that same house. God's house has no dividing walls or closed doors. 'I am the door,' Jesus says. 'Anyone who enters through me will be safe' (John 10:9). The more fully we enter into the house of love, the more clearly we see that we are there together with all humanity and that in and through Christ we are brothers and sisters, members of one family. (L, p. 48)

Salve Regina

Hail, holy Queen, Mother of mercy …

Bible Before Bed

Who among you delights in life,
Longs for time to enjoy prosperity?
Guard your tongue from evil,
Your lips from any breath of deceit.
Turn away from evil and do good,
Seek peace and pursue it.
For the eyes of the Lord are on the upright,
His ear turned to their cry.
But the Lord's face is set
Against those who do evil.

(Psalm 34:13–16)

THURSDAY

Vigils

Today I imagined my inner self as a place crowded with pins and needles. How could I receive anyone in my prayer when there is no real place for them to be free and relaxed? When I am still so full of preoccupations, jealousies, angry feelings, anyone who enters will get hurt. I had a very vivid realization that I must create some free space in my innermost self so that I may indeed invite others to enter and be healed. To pray for others means to offer others a hospitable place where I can really listen to their needs and pains. Compassion, therefore, calls for a self-scrutiny that can lead to inner gentleness. (G, p. 145)

Lauds

Once, while visiting a dying friend, I directly

experienced the holy emptiness. In my friend's presence I felt no desire to ask questions about the past or to speculate about the future. We were just together without fear, without guilt or shame, without worries. In that emptiness, God's unconditional love could be sensed and we could say what the old Simeon said when he took the Christ child in his arms: 'Now, Master, you can let your servant go in peace as you promised.' There, in the midst of the dreadful emptiness, was complete trust, complete peace, and complete joy. Death no longer was the enemy. Love was victorious. (PS, p. 133)

Angelus
The Angel of the Lord brought tidings to Mary …

None
Although the discipline of solitude asks us to set aside time and space, what finally matters is that our hearts become like quiet cells where

God can dwell, wherever we go and whatever we do. The more we train ourselves to spend time with God and him alone, the more we will discover that God is with us at all times and in all places. Then we will be able to recognize him even in the midst of a busy and active life ... Thus the discipline of solitude enables us to live active lives in the world, while remaining always in the presence of the living God. (MATN, pp. 79–81)

Vespers

There is great pain and suffering in the world. But the pain hardest to bear is your own. Once you have taken up that cross, you will be able to see clearly the crosses that others have to bear, and you will be able to reveal to them their own ways to joy, peace, and freedom. (IVL, p. 88)

Compline

We need new eyes to see and new ears to hear

the truth of our unity, a unity which cannot be perceived by our broken, sinful, anxious hearts. Only a heart filled with perfect love can perceive the unity of humanity. This requires divine perception. God sees his people as one, as belonging to the same family and living in the same house. God wants to share this divine perception with us. By sending the only beloved son to live and die for us all, God wants to open our eyes so that we can see that we belong together in the embrace of God's perfect love. (L, p. 46)

Salve Regina
Hail, holy Queen, Mother of mercy …

Bible Before Bed
Again, do not listen to all that people say, then
   you will not hear your servant abusing you.
For often, as you very well know, you have
   abused others. (Ecclesiastes 7:21–2)

FRIDAY

Vigils

Every time we enter into solitude we withdraw from our windy, tornadolike, fiery lives and we open ourselves for the great encounter, the meeting with Love. But first in our solitude is the discovery of our own restlessness, our drivenness, our compulsiveness, our urge to act quickly, to make an impact, and to have influence. We really have to try very hard to withstand the gnawing urge to return as quickly as possible to the work of 'relevance.' But when we persevere with the help of a gentle discipline, we slowly come to hear the still, small voice and to feel the delicate breeze, and so come to know the presence of Love. (CR, pp. 27–8)

Lauds

The word 'Eucharist' means literally 'act of

thanksgiving.' To celebrate the Eucharist and to live a Eucharistic life has everything to do with gratitude. Living Eucharistically is living life as a gift, a gift for which one is grateful. But gratitude is not the most obvious response to life, certainly not when we experience life as a series of losses! Still, the great mystery we celebrate in the Eucharist and live in a Eucharistic life is precisely that through mourning our losses we come to know life as a gift. The beauty and preciousness of life is intimately linked with its fragility and mortality. We can experience that every day – when we take a flower in our hands, when we see a butterfly dance in the air, when we caress a little baby. Fragility and giftedness are both there, and our joy is connected with both. (WBH, p. 30)

Angelus
The Angel of the Lord brought tidings to Mary …

None

Open wounds stink and do not heal. Making one's own wounds a source of healing, therefore, does not call for a sharing of superficial personal pain but for a constant willingness to see one's own pain and suffering as rising from the depth of the human condition which all men share. (WBH, p. 88)

Vespers

Anyone who wants to pay attention without intention has to be at home in his own house – that is, he has to discover the center of his life in his own heart. Concentration, which leads to meditation and contemplation, is therefore the necessary precondition for true hospitality. When our souls are restless, when we are driven by thousands of different and often conflicting stimuli, when we are always 'over there' between people, ideas and worries of this world, how can we possibly create the room and space where someone else can enter freely

without feeling himself an unlawful intruder?
(WBH, p. 90)

Compline

Communion with Jesus means becoming like
him. With him we are nailed on the cross, with
him we are laid in the tomb, with him we are
raised up to accompany lost travelers on their
journey. Communion, becoming Christ, leads
us to a new realm of being. It ushers us into the
Kingdom. There the old distinctions between
happiness and sadness, success, and failure,
praise and blame, health and sickness, life and
death no longer exist. There we no longer
belong to the world that keeps dividing,
judging, separating, and evaluating. There we
belong to Christ and Christ to us, and with
Christ we belong to God. (WBH, p. 74)

Salve Regina

Hail, holy Queen, Mother of mercy …

Bible Before Bed

The message of the cross is folly for those who are on the way to ruin, but for those of us who are on the road to salvation, it the power of God. (1 Corinthians 1:18)

SATURDAY

Vigils

Prayer is not introspection. It is not a scrupulous, inward-looking analysis of our own thoughts and feelings but is an attentiveness to the Presence of Love personified inviting us to an encounter. Prayer is the presentation of our thoughts – reflective, as well as daydreams, and night dreams – to the One who receives them, sees them in the light of unconditional love, and responds to them with divine compassion. (CR, p. 69)

Lauds

Each Eucharist begins with a cry for God's mercy. There is probably no prayer in the history of Christianity that has been prayed so frequently and intimately as the prayer 'Lord, have mercy.' It is the prayer that not only stands at the beginning of all Eucharistic liturgies of the West but also sounds as an ongoing cry through all Eastern liturgies. Lord, have mercy, *Kyrie Eleison, Gospody Pomiloe.* It's the cry of God's people, the cry of people with a contrite heart. (WBH, p. 31)

Angelus
The Angel of the Lord brought tidings to Mary …

None
Is there a third way, a Christian way? It is my growing conviction that in Jesus the mystical and the revolutionary ways are not opposites, but two sides of the same human mode of experiential transcendence. I am increasingly convinced that conversion is the individual equivalent of revolution. Therefore every real revolutionary is challenged to be a mystic at heart, and he who walks the mystical way is called to unmask the illusory quality of human

[49]

society. Mysticism and revolution are two aspects of the same attempt to bring about radical change. No mystic can prevent himself from becoming a social critic, since in self-reflection he will discover the roots of a sick society. Similarly, no revolutionary can avoid facing his own human condition, since in the midst of his struggle for a new world he will find that he is also fighting his own reactionary fears and false ambitions. (WBH, p. 19)

Vespers
Jesus is God-for-us, God-with-us, God-with-in-us. Jesus is God giving himself completely, pouring himself out for us without reserve. Jesus doesn't hold back or cling to his own possessions. He gives all there is to give. 'Eat, drink, this is my body, this is my blood … this is me for you!' (WBH, p. 67)

Compline
Contemplative life, as Evagrius describes it, is a

life that leads us to see our world as a transparent world, a world that points beyond itself. Finding God in prayer reveals the true nature of our world to us. Just as a window cannot be a real window for us if we cannot look through it, so our world cannot show to us its real identity if it remains opaque and does not point beyond itself. You and I, on a seeking journey, must therefore try to move continuously from opaqueness to transparency in three central relationships with nature, with time, and with people. (CR, p. 86)

Salve Regina
Hail, holy Queen, Mother of mercy …

Bible Before Bed
When I call, answer me, God, upholder of my
    right.
In my distress you have set me at large;
Take pity on me and hear my prayer!

(Psalms 4:1)

WEEK TWO

SUNDAY

Vigils

To the degree in which our loneliness is converted into solitude we can move from hostility to hospitality. There obviously is no question of chronology. The complex and subtle movements of the inner life cannot be neatly divided. But it remains true that loneliness often leads to hostile behavior and that solitude is the climate of hospitality. (RO, p. 102)

Lauds

Holding the cup of life means looking critically at what we are living. This requires great courage, because when we start looking, we might be terrified by what we see. Questions may arise that we don't know how to answer. Doubts may come up about things we thought we were sure about. Fear may emerge from unexpected places. We are tempted to say: 'Let's just live life. All this thinking about it only makes things harder.' Still, we intuitively know that without looking at life critically we lose our vision and our direction. When we drink the cup without holding it first, we may simply get drunk and wander around aimlessly. (CDC, p. 27)

Angelus

The angel of the Lord brought tidings to Mary
And she conceived of the Holy Spirit.

Hail, Mary full of grace, the Lord is with thee: Blessed art thou among women, and blessed is The fruit of thy womb, Jesus. Holy Mary, Mother of God, pray for us sinners, now and at the hour of our death. Amen.

Behold the handmaid of the Lord:
Be it done unto me according to your word.

Hail, Mary …

And the Word was made flesh:
And dwelt among us.

Hail, Mary …

Pray for us, O holy Mother of God:
That we may be made worthy of the promises
   of Christ.

We beseech thee, O Lord, to pour thy grace into
our hearts, that as we have known the incarnation of thy Son Jesus Christ by the message of
an angel, so by his cross and passion we may be
brought to the glory of his resurrection, through
the same Christ our Lord.

None
Adam's death: I couldn't keep my eyes away
from him. I thought, here is the man who more
than anyone has connected me with God and

the Daybreak community. Here is the man whom I cared for during my first year at Daybreak and have come to love so much. Here is the one I have written about, talked about all over Canada and the United States ... Here is Adam, my friend, my beloved friend, the most vulnerable of all the people I have ever known and at the same time the most powerful. He is dead now. (SJ, p. 105)

Vespers

Prayer is the ongoing cry of the incarnate Lord to the loving God. It is eternity in the midst of mortality, life among death, hope in the midst of despair, true promise surrounded by lies. Prayer brings love alive among us. So let us pray unceasingly. (SJs, p. 15)

Compline

O Lord Jesus, I look at you, and my eyes are fixed on your eyes. Your eyes penetrate the eternal mystery of the divine and see the glory of God. They are also the eyes that saw Simon, Andrew, Nathanael and Levi, the eyes that saw the woman with a hemorrhage, the widow of Nain, the blind, the lame, the lepers, and the hungry crowd, the eyes that saw the sad, rich ruler, the fearful disciples on the lake, and the sorrowful women at the tomb. Your eyes, O Lord, see in one glance the inexhaustible love of God and the seemingly endless agony of all people who have lost faith in that love and are like sheep without a shepherd. (SJs, p. 335)

Salve Regina

Hail, holy Queen, Mother of mercy,
Our life, our sweetness and our hope.
To thee do we cry,
Poor banished children of Eve,
To thee do we send up our sighs,
Mourning and weeping
In this valley of tears.
Turn then, most gracious Advocate,
Thine eyes of mercy toward us,

And after this our exile,
Show unto us the blessed fruit
Of thy womb, Jesus.
O clement, O loving,
O sweet Virgin Mary!
Pray for us, O Holy Mother of God,
That we may be made worthy
Of the promises of Christ.
Amen.

Bible Before Bed

Yahweh is my shepherd, I lack nothing.
In grassy meadows he lets me lie.
By tranquil streams he leads me
To restore my spirit.
He guides me in paths of saving justice
As befits his name. (Psalm 23:1–3)

MONDAY

Vigils

Healing means first of all allowing strangers to become sensitive and obedient to their own stories. Healers, therefore, become students who want to learn, and patients become teachers who want to teach. Just as teachers learn their course material best during the preparation and ordering of their ideas for presentation to students, so patients learn their own story by telling it to a healer who wants to hear it. Healers are hosts who patiently and carefully listen to the story of the suffering strangers. (RO, p. 96)

Lauds

Now I look at the man of sorrows. He hangs on a cross with outstretched arms. It is Jesus, condemned by Pontius Pilate, crucified by

Roman soldiers, and ridiculed by Jews and Gentiles alike. But it is also us, the whole human race, people of all times and all places, uprooted from the earth as a spectacle of agony for the entire universe to watch. 'When I am lifted up from the earth,' Jesus said, 'I shall draw all people to myself' (John 12:32). Jesus, the man of sorrow, and we, the people of sorrow, hang there between heaven and earth, crying out, 'God, our God, why have you forsaken us?' (CDC, p. 35)

Angelus

The angel of the Lord brought tidings to Mary …

None

So what about my life of prayer? Do I like to pray? Do I want to pray? Do I spend time praying? Frankly, the answer is no to all three questions. After sixty-three years of life and thirty-eight years of priesthood, my prayer seems as dead as a rock. I remember fondly my teenage years, when I could hardly stay away from the church. For hours I would stay on my knees filled with a deep sense of Jesus' presence. I couldn't believe that not everyone wanted to pray ... Are the darkness and dryness of my prayer signs of God's absence, or are they signs of a presence deeper and wider than my senses can contain? (SJ, p. 5)

Vespers

True prayer always includes becoming poor. When we pray we stand naked and vulnerable in front of Our Lord and show him our true condition. If one were to do this not just for oneself, but in the name of thousands of surrounding poor people, wouldn't that be 'mission' in the true sense of being sent into the world as Jesus himself was sent into the world? To lift up your hands to the Lord and show him the hungry children who play on the dusty streets, the tired women who carry their babies on their backs to the marketplace, the men who try to forget their misery by drinking too much beer on the weekends, the jobless teenagers and the homeless squatters, together with their laughter, friendly gestures, and gentle words – wouldn't that be true service? (SJs, p. 157)

Compline

One thing is becoming clear to me: God became flesh for us to show us that the way to come in touch with God's love is the human way, in which the limited and partial affection that people can give offers access to the un-limited and complete love that God has poured into the human heart. God's love cannot be found outside this human affection, even when that human affection is tainted by the broken-ness of our time. (SJs, p. 337)

Salve Regina

Hail, holy Queen, Mother of mercy …

Bible Before Bed

Then he took bread, and when he had given thanks, he broke it and gave it to them, saying, 'This is my body given for you; do this in remembrance of me.' (Luke 22:19)

TUESDAY

Vigils

As healers we have to receive the story of our fellow human beings with a compassionate heart, a heart that does not judge or condemn but recognizes how the stranger's story connects with our own. We have to offer safe boundaries within which the often painful past can be revealed and the search for a new life can find a start. (RO, p. 96)

Lauds

In the midst of the sorrows is consolation, in the midst of the darkness is light, in the midst of the despair is hope, in the midst of Babylon is a glimpse of Jerusalem, and in the midst of the army of demons is the consoling angel. The cup of sorrow, inconceivable as it seems, is also the cup of joy. Only when we discover this in

our own life can we consider drinking it.
(CDC, p. 38)

Angelus

The Angel of the Lord brought tidings to
Mary …

None

Jesus said to his disciples, 'A little while, and
you will no longer see me, and again a little
while, and you will see me' (John 16:16). Life is
'a little while,' a short moment of waiting. But
life is not empty waiting. It is to wait full of
expectation. The knowledge that God will
indeed fulfill the promise to renew everything,
and will offer us a 'new heaven and a new
earth' makes the waiting exciting. (SJ, p. 166)

Vespers

The great paradox of ministry, therefore, is that
we minister above all with our weakness, a
weakness that invites us to receive from those

to whom we go. The more in touch we are with our own need for healing and salvation, the more open we are to receive in gratitude what others have to offer us. The true skill of ministry is to help fearful and often oppressed men and women become aware of their own gifts, by receiving them in gratitude. In that sense, ministry becomes the skill of active dependency: willing to be dependent on what others have to give but often do not realize they have. (SJS, p. 163)

Compline

This is a very encouraging thought. God does not require a pure heart before embracing us. Even if we return only because following our desires has failed to bring happiness, God will take us back. Even if we return because being a Christian brings us more peace than being a pagan, God will receive us. Even if we return because our sins did not offer as much satisfaction as we had hoped, God will take us back.

Even if we return because we could not make it on our own, God will receive us. God's love does not require any explanations about why we are returning. God is glad to see us home and wants to give us all we desire, just for being home. (SJ, pp. 35–6)

Salve Regina
Hail, holy Queen, Mother of mercy …

Bible Before Bed
'In the same way, I tell you, there will be more rejoicing in heaven over one sinner repenting than over ninety-nine upright people who have no need of repentance.' (Luke 15:7)

WEDNESDAY

Vigils

What keeps us from opening ourselves to the reality of the world? Could it be that we cannot accept our powerlessness and are only willing to see those wounds that we can heal?

Could it be that we do not want to give up our illusion that we are masters over our world and, therefore, create our own Disneyland where we can make ourselves believe that all events of life are safely under control? (RO, p. 57)

Lauds

Joys are hidden in sorrows! I know this from my own times of depression. I know it from living with people with mental handicaps. I know it from looking into the eyes of patients, and from being with the poorest of the poor. We keep forgetting this truth and become overwhelmed by our own darkness. We easily lose sight of our joys and speak of our sorrow as the only reality there is. (CDC, p. 50)

Angelus
The angel of the Lord brought tidings to Mary …

None
I have made an inner decision to keep looking at Jesus as the one who calls us to the heart of God, a heart that knows only love. It is from that perspective that I reflect on everything Jesus says, including his harsh statements. Jesus created divisions, but I have chosen to believe that these divisions were the result not of intolerance or fanaticism but of his radical call to love, forgive, and be reconciled. (SJ, p. 127)

Vespers
Jesus learned obedience from what he suffered. This means that the pains and struggles of

which Jesus became part made him listen more perfectly to God. In and through his sufferings, he came to know God and could respond to his call. Maybe there are no better words than these to summarize the meaning of the option for the poor. Entering into suffering of the poor is the way to become obedient, that is, a listener to God. Suffering accepted and shared in love breaks down our selfish defenses and sets us free to accept God's guidance. (SJs, p. 287)

Compline

To return to God means to return to God with all that I am and all that I have. I cannot return to God with just half of my being. As I reflected this morning again on the story of the prodigal son and tried to experience myself in the embrace of the father, I suddenly felt a certain resistance to being embraced so fully and totally. I experienced not only a desire to be embraced but also a fear of losing my independence. I realized that God's love is a jealous love. God wants not just a part of me, but all of me. (SJs, p. 346)

Salve Regina
Hail, holy Queen, Mother of mercy …

Bible Before Bed
The father said, 'My son, you are with me always and all I have is yours.' (Luke 15:31)

ThURSDAY

Vigils

The French author Simone Weil writes in her notebooks: 'Waiting patiently in expectation is the foundation of the spiritual life.' With these words she expresses powerfully how absence and presence are never separated when we reach out to God in prayer. The spiritual life is, first of all, a patient waiting, that is, a waiting in suffering, during which the many experiences of unfulfillment remind us of God's absence. (RO, p. 128)

Lauds

True sanctity is precisely drinking our own cup and trusting that by thus fully claiming our own, irreplaceable journey, we can become a source of hope for many. Vincent van Gogh, miserable and brokenhearted as he was, believed without question in his vocation to paint, and he went as far as he could with what little he had. This is true for Francis of Assisi, Dorothy Day of New York, and Oscar Romero of San Salvador. Small people, but great in drinking their cups to the full. (CDC, p. 83)

Angelus
The Angel of the Lord brought tidings to Mary ...

None
Every time I have an opportunity to create understanding between people and foster moments of healing, forgiving, and uniting, I will try to do it, even thought I might be criticized as too soft, too bending, too appeasing. Is this desire a lack of fervor and zeal for the truth? Is it an unwillingness to be a martyr? Is it spinelessness? I am not always sure what comes from my weakness and what comes from my strength ... But I have to trust that,

after sixty-four years of life, I have some ground to stand on, a ground where Jesus stands with me. (SJ, p. 127)

Vespers

God came to us because he wanted to join us on the road, to listen to our story, and to help us realize that we are not walking in circles but moving towards the house of peace and joy. This is the great mystery of Christmas that continues to give us comfort and consolation: we are not alone on our journey. The God of love who gave us life sent us his only Son to be with us at all times and in all places, so that we never have to feel lost in our struggles but always can trust that he walks with us. (SJs, p. 211)

Compline

Prayer heals. Not just the answer to prayer. When we give up our competition with God and offer God every part of our heart, holding back nothing at all, we come to know God's love for us and discover how safe we are in his embrace. Once we know again that God has not rejected us, but keeps us close to his heart, we can find again the joy of living, even though God might guide our life in a different direction from our desires. (SJs, p. 377)

Salve Regina
Hail, holy Queen, Mother of mercy …

Bible Before Bed
'Ask, and it will be given to you; search, and you will find; knock and the door will be opened to you.' (Matthew 7:7)

FRIDAY

Vigils

While the movement from loneliness to solitude makes us reach out to our innermost self, the movement from hostility to hospitality makes us reach out to others. The term hospitality was used only to come to a better insight into the nature of a mature Christian relationship to our fellow human beings … To help, to serve, to care, to guide, to heal, these words were all used to express a reaching out toward our neighbor whereby we perceive life as a gift not to possess but to share. (RO, p. 109)

Lauds

The cup that Jesus speaks about is neither a symbol of victory nor a symbol of death. It is a symbol of life, filled with sorrows and joys that we can hold, lift, and drink as a blessing and a way to salvation. 'Can you drink the cup that I am going to drink?' Jesus asks us. It is the question that will have a different meaning every day of our lives. Can we embrace fully the sorrows and joys that come to us day after day? (CDC, p. 104)

Angelus
The Angel of the Lord brought tidings to Mary …

None
What to do with this inner wound that is so easily touched and starts bleeding again? It is such a familiar wound. It has been with me for many years. I don't think this wound – this immense need for affection, and this immense fear of rejection – will ever go away. It is there to stay, but maybe for a good reason. Perhaps it is a gateway to my salvation, a door to glory, and a passage to freedom! (SJ, p. 25)

Vespers

The challenge is to let God be who he wants
to be. A part of us clings to our aloneness and
does not allow God to touch us where we are
most in pain. Often we hide from him precisely
those places in ourselves where we feel guilty,
ashamed, confused, and lost. Thus we do not
give him a chance to be with us where we felt
most alone. (SJs, p. 211)

Compline

I am convinced that we can choose joy. Every
moment we can decide to respond to an event
or a person with joy instead of sadness. When
we truly believe that God is life and only life,
then nothing need have the power to draw us
into the sad realm of death. To choose joy does
not mean to choose happy feelings or an
artificial atmosphere of hilarity. But it does
mean the determination to let whatever takes
place bring us one step closer to the God of
life. (SJs, p. 390)

Salve Regina
Hail, holy Queen, Mother of mercy …

Bible Before Bed
'Do not store up treasures for yourselves on earth, where moth and woodworm destroy them and thieves can break in and steal. But store up treasures for yourselves in heaven where neither moth nor woodworm destroys them and thieves cannot break in and steal. For wherever your treasure is, there will your heart be too.' (Matthew 6:19–21)

SATURDAY

Vigils

From the point of a Christian spirituality, it is important to stress that every human being is called upon to be a healer. Although there are many professions asking for special long and arduous training, we can never leave the task of healing to the specialist. In fact, the specialists can only retain their humanity in their work when they see their professions as a form of service which they carry out, not instead of, but as part of, the whole people of God. (RO, p. 93)

Lauds

Jesus didn't throw the cup away in despair. No, he kept it in his hands, willing to drink it to the dregs. This was not a show of willpower, staunch determination, or great heroism. This was a deep spiritual yes to Abba, the lover of his wounded heart. (CDC, p. 37)

Angelus
The Angel of the Lord brought tidings to Mary …

None
The kingdom of God is at hand, at our fingertips. Jesus calls us to repent, which means to have a contrite heart, a heart broken open by the plow of suffering, a heart able to receive the seed of the Kingdom, a heart able to see the treasure in the field, a heart capable of hearing the soft voice of love. Even though we live in a violent world, full of hatred and war, we can already enter the Kingdom now and belong to a community of faith, hope, and love. (SJ, p. 207)

Vespers
Every time I have the courage or gave others the courage to face their blindness, their mental

anguish, or their spiritual agony and let other become part of the struggle, new creative energies became available and the basis of community was laid. Fear, shame, and guilt often make us stay in our isolation and prevent us from realizing that our handicap, whatever it is, can always become the way to an intimate and healing fellowship in which we come to know one another as humans. (SJs, p. 205)

Compline

It is not easy to let the voice of God's mercy speak to us because it is a voice asking for an always open relationship, one in which sins are acknowledged, forgiveness received, and love renewed. It does not offer us a solution, but a friendship. It does not take away our problems, but promises not to avoid them. It does not tell us where it all will end, but assures us that we will never be alone. A true relationship is hard work because loving is hard work, with many tears and many smiles.

But it is God's work and worth every part of it. (SJs, p. 403)

Salve Regina
Hail, holy Queen, Mother of mercy …

Bible Before Bed
'Be compassionate just as your Father is compassionate. Do not judge, and you will not be judged; do not condemn, and you will not be condemned; forgive, and you will be forgiven. Give, and there will be gifts for you: a full measure, pressed down, shaken together, and overflowing, will be poured into your lap; because the standard you use will be the standard used for you.' (Luke 6: 36–8)

WEEK THREE

SUNDAY

Vigils

Somewhere deep in our hearts we already know that success, fame, influence, power, and money do not give us the inner joy and peace we crave. Somewhere we can even sense a certain envy of those who have shed all false ambitions and found a deeper fulfillment in their relationship with God. Yes, somewhere we can even get a taste of that mysterious joy in the smile of those who have nothing to lose. (SWC, pp. 34–5)

Lauds

When a person is able to thank he is able to know his limitations without feeling defensive and to be self-confident without being proud. He claims his own powers and at the same time he confesses his need for help. Thanking in a

[89]

real sense avoids submissiveness as well as possessiveness. It is the act of a free man who can say: I thank you. (I, p. 58)

Angelus

The angel of the Lord brought tidings to Mary
And she conceived of the Holy Spirit.

Hail, Mary full of grace, the Lord is with thee: Blessed art thou among women, and blessed is The fruit of thy womb, Jesus. Holy Mary, Mother of God, pray for us sinners, now and at the hour of our death. Amen.

Behold the handmaid of the Lord:
Be it done unto me according to your word.

Hail, Mary …

And the Word was made flesh:
And dwelt among us.

Hail, Mary …

Pray for us, O holy Mother of God:
That we may be made worthy of the promises
   of Christ.

We beseech thee, O Lord, to pour thy grace into
our hearts, that as we have known the incarnation of thy Son Jesus Christ by the message of
an angel, so by his cross and passion we may be
brought to the glory of his resurrection, through
the same Christ our Lord.

None

To be chosen as the Beloved of God is something radically different. Instead of excluding
others, it includes others. Instead of rejecting
others as less valuable, it accepts others in their
own uniqueness. It is not a competitive, but a
compassionate choice. Our minds have great
difficulty in coming to grips with such a reality.
Maybe our minds will never understand it.
Perhaps it is only our hearts that can accomplish this. (LB, pp. 55–6)

Vespers

Solitude is the furnace of transformation. Without solitude we remain victims of our society and continue to be entangled in the illusions of the false self. Jesus himself entered into this furnace. There he was tempted with the three compulsions of the world: to be relevant ('turn stones into loaves'), to be spectacular ('throw yourself down'), and to be powerful ('I will give you all these kingdoms'). (WH, p. 25)

Compline

Every time you listen with great attentiveness to the voice that calls you the Beloved, you will discover within yourself a desire to hear that voice longer and more deeply. It is like discovering a well in the desert. Once you have touched fertile ground, you want to dig deeper. This digging and searching for an underground stream is the discipline of prayer. (SD, p. 34)

Salve Regina

Hail, holy Queen, Mother of mercy,
Our life, our sweetness and our hope.
To thee do we cry,
Poor banished children of Eve,
To thee do we send up our sighs,
Mourning and weeping
In this valley of tears.
Turn then, most gracious Advocate,
Thine eyes of mercy toward us,
And after this our exile,
Show unto us the blessed fruit
Of thy womb, Jesus.
O clement, O loving,
O sweet Virgin Mary!
Pray for us, O Holy Mother of God,
That we may be made worthy
Of the promises of Christ.
Amen.

Bible Before Bed

'The kingdom of Heaven is like a treasure

hidden in a field which someone has found; he hides it again, goes off in his joy, sells everything he owns and buys the field.'

(Matthew 13:44)

MONDAY

Vigils
The downward way is God's way, not ours.
God is revealed as God to us in the downward
pull, because only the One who is God can be
emptied of divine privileges and become as we
are. The great mystery upon which our faith
rests is that the One who is in no way like us,
who cannot be compared with us, nor enter
into competition with us, has come among us
and taken on our mortal flesh. (SWC, p. 38)

Lauds
Help me find and cherish myself – to solve the
problems of myself and others, to more clearly
see the direction in which I'm going. It has
been so cloudy and jerky – sometimes I wonder if I'm progressing at all – and sometimes I
wonder if I can. Remove this doubt I have

about myself – or better let me see the doubt and lack of confidence for what is it, and in removing it, learn more of it. (I, p. 45)

Angelus
The Angel of the Lord brought tidings to Mary …

None
In the midst of this extremely painful reality, we have to dare to reclaim the truth that we are God's chosen ones, even when our world does not choose us. As long as we allow our parents, siblings, teachers, friends, and lovers to determine whether we are chosen or not, we are caught in the net of a suffocating world that accepts or rejects us according to its own agenda of effectiveness and control. (LB, p. 57)

Vespers
In solitude I get rid of my scaffolding: no friends to talk with, no telephone calls to make,

no meetings to attend, no music to entertain, no books to distract, just me – naked, vulnerable, weak, sinful, deprived, broken – nothing. It is this nothingness that I have to face in my solitude, a nothingness so dreadful that everything in me wants to run to my friends, my work, and my distractions so that I can forget my nothingness and make myself believe that I am worth something. (WH, p. 27)

Compline

If I am the Beloved of God, how do I claim my Belovedness? I begin by daily repeating the very words Jesus heard at his baptism, for they are also meant for me and for you: 'You are my Beloved. With you I am well pleased.' Spend a few minutes every day in prayer, meditating on God's great love. (SD, p. 35)

Salve Regina

Hail, holy Queen, Mother of mercy …

Bible Before Bed

And when Jesus had been baptised he at once
came up from the water, and suddenly the
heavens opened and he saw the Spirit of God
descending like a dove and coming down on
him. And suddenly there was a voice from
heaven, 'This is my son, the Beloved; my favour
rests on him.' (Matthew 3:6–7)

TUESDAY

Vigils

The spiritual life is the life of the Spirit of Christ in us, a life that sets us free to be strong while weak, to be free while captive, to be joyful while in pain, to be rich while poor, to be on the downward way of salvation while living in the midst of an upwardly mobile society. (SWC, p. 44)

Lauds

Lord, I don't really feel like praying. I'm confused, everything is confused. I don't know what I'll be doing next year – I don't even know for sure what I want to be doing next year, or what I should be doing. I feel guilty praying – turning to you at a time like this because I feel two-faced to pray only when I need help and not to pray when I don't. (I, pp. 45–6)

Angelus

The Angel of the Lord brought tidings to Mary …

None

Our brokenness is truly ours. Nobody else's. Our brokenness is as unique as our chosenness and our blessedness. The way we are broken is as much an expression of our individuality as the way we are taken and blessed. Yes, fearsome as it may sound, as the Beloved ones, we are called to claim our unique brokenness, just as we have to claim our unique chosenness and our unique blessedness. (LB, p. 88)

Vespers

Solitude is thus the place of purification and transformation, the place of the great struggle and the great encounter. Solitude is not simply a means to an end. Solitude is its own end. It is the place where Christ remodels us in his own image and frees us from the victimizing compulsions of the world. (WH, p. 32)

Compline

There is so much fear and agony in us. Fear of people, fear of God, and much raw, undefined, free-floating anxiety. I wonder if fear is not our main obstacle to prayer. When we enter into the presence of God and start to sense that huge reservoir of fear in us, we want to run away into the many distractions that our busy world offers us so abundantly. (SD, p. 58)

Salve Regina

Hail, holy Queen, Mother of mercy ...

Bible Before Bed

'This is my Son, the Beloved; he enjoys my favour. Listen to him.' When they heard this, the disciples fell on their faces, overcome with fear. But Jesus came up and touched them, saying, 'Stand up, do not be afraid.' And when they raised their eyes they saw no one but Jesus. (Matthew 17: 5–8)

WEDNESDAY

Vigils
To be a Christian who is willing to travel with
Christ on his downward road requires being
willing to detach oneself constantly from any
need to be relevant, and to trust ever more
deeply the Word of God. Thus, we do not resist
the temptation to be relevant by doing
irrelevant things but by clinging to the Word
of God who is the source of all relevancy.
(SWC, pp. 52–3)

Lauds
We want to be ambitious and competitive but
sometimes we want to forgive. We want
strength and successes, but sometimes we feel a
desire to confess our other side. We want to
kill, but also to cure, to hurt but also to help.
Although the world in which we live keeps

suggesting that realism is an outlook on life based on power, confusing but at the same time attractive prophets keep saying that there is another possible alternative, the alternative of love. (I, p. 33)

Angelus
The Angel of the Lord brought tidings to Mary …

None
Our greatest fulfillment lies in giving ourselves to others. Although it often seems people give only to receive, I believe, that, beyond all our desires to be appreciated, rewarded, and acknowledged, there lies a simple and pure desire to give. I remember how I once spent long hours looking in Dutch stores for a birthday gift for my father or mother, simply enjoying being able to give. Our humanity comes to its fullest bloom in giving. (LB, p. 106)

Vespers
In solitude we realize that nothing human is alien to us, that the roots of all conflict, war, injustice, cruelty, hatred, jealousy, and envy are deeply anchored in our own heart. In solitude our hearts of stone can be turned into a heart of flesh, a rebellious heart into a contrite heart, and a closed heart into a heart that can open itself to all suffering people in a gesture of solidarity. (WH, p. 34)

Compline
To pray unceasingly, as St. Paul asks us to do, would be completely impossible if it meant to think constantly about or speak continuously to God. To pray unceasingly does not mean to think about God in contrast to thinking about other things, or to talk to God instead of talking to other people. Rather, it means to think, speak, and live in the presence of God. (SD, p. 61)

Salve Regina
Hail, holy Queen, Mother of mercy …

Bible Before Bed
'In truth I tell you once again, if two of you on earth agree to ask anything at all, it will be granted to you by my Father in heaven. For where two or three meet in my name, I am there among them.' (Matthew 18:19–20)

THURSDAY

Vigils
This experience of God's acceptance frees us from our needy self and thus creates new space where we can pay selfless attention to others. This new freedom in Christ allows us to move in the world uninhibited by our compulsions and to act creatively even when we are laughed at and rejected, even when our words and actions lead us to death. (SWC, p. 58)

Lauds
Love is not based on the willingness to listen, to understand problems of others or to tolerate their otherness. Love is based on the mutuality of the confession our total self to each other. This makes us free to declare not only: 'My strength is your strength,' but also: 'Your pain is my pain, your weakness is my weakness, your

sin is my sin.' It is in this intimate fellowship of the weak that love is born. (I, p. 29)

Angelus
The Angel of the Lord brought tidings to Mary …

None
We are chosen, blessed, and broken to be given, not only in life, but in death as well. As the Beloved Children of God, we are called to become bread for each other — bread for the world. (LB, p. 121)

Vespers
Christians have tried to practice silence as the way to self-control. Clearly silence is a discipline needed in many different situations: in teaching and learning, in preaching and worship, in visiting and counseling. Silence is a very concrete, practical, and useful discipline in all our ministerial tasks … Silence is solitude practiced in action. (WH, p. 44)

Compline

As we learn how to pray, somewhere along the way we experience the crying out to God about our needs as a monologue, a one-sided affair. And even when prayer becomes a dialogue, with God speaking and answering our prayers, we long for more of God's presence. The truth is that prayer is more than feeling, speaking, thinking, and conversing with God. To pray means to be quiet and listen, whether or not we feel God is speaking to us. (SD, p. 63)

Salve Regina

Hail, holy Queen, Mother of mercy …

Bible Before Bed

Jesus answered, 'Have faith in God. In truth I tell you, if anyone says to this mountain, "Be pulled up and thrown into the sea," with no doubt in his heart that what he says will happen, it will be done for him.' (Mark 11:23)

FRIDAY

Vigils

Through a disciplined life of contemplative prayer we slowly can come to realize God's original love, the love that existed long before we could love ourselves or receive any other human love. The apostle John says: 'Love comes from God ... because God is love. We are to love, then, because God loved us first' (1 John 4:7–8, 19). (SWC, pp. 58–9)

Lauds

The unfathomable mystery of God is that God is a Lover who wants to be loved. The one who created us is waiting for our response to the love that gave us our being. God not only says, 'You are my Beloved.' God also asks: 'Do you love me?' and offers countless chances to say 'Yes.' (LB, p. 133)

Angelus
The Angel of the Lord brought tidings to Mary ...

None
Compassion is hard because it requires the inner disposition to go with others to the place where they are weak, vulnerable, lonely, and broken. But this is not our spontaneous response to suffering. What we desire most is to do away with suffering by fleeing from it or finding a quick cure for it ... This means first and foremost doing something to show that our presence makes a difference. (WH, p. 34)

Vespers
Words can only create communion and thus new life when they embody the silence from which they emerge. As soon as we begin to take hold of each other by our words, and use words to defend ourselves or offend others, the word no longer speaks of silence. But when the

word calls forth the healing and restoring stillness of its own silence, few words are needed: much can be said without being spoken. (WH, p. 57)

Compline
Truly the good news is that God is not a distant God, a God to be feared and avoided, a God of revenge, but a God who is moved by our pains and participates in the fullness of the human struggle. God is a compassionate God. This means, first of all, that God is a God who has chosen to be with us. As soon as we call God, 'God-with-us,' we enter into a new relationship of intimacy. (SD, p. 74)

Salve Regina
Hail, holy Queen, Mother of mercy …

Bible Before Bed
'You must love the Lord your God with all your heart, with all your soul, with all your

mind and with all your strength ... You must love your neighbour as yourself. There is no commandment greater than these.'

(Mark 12:30–1)

SATURDAY

Vigils

Meditation thus is much more than thinking about the words of Scripture, much more than trying to understand the parables, or analyzing complicated sayings. Meditation is the growing inner availability to the word so that the Word can guide us, can open us, can remove our fears, and come to dwell in us. True meditation is thus letting the Word become flesh in us. (SWC, pp. 79–80)

Lauds

Your mistakes, failures and offenses are unchangeable elements on the record of your life. Evil then is definitive and unchangeable. The only solution for the irreversible is its destruction. If evil cannot be reversed and forgiven, the only thing those living in the taking mode can do with it is to cut it out, to uproot it, to burn it to ashes. (I, p. 27)

Angelus

The Angel of the Lord brought tidings to Mary ...

None

Spiritually we do not belong to the world. And this is precisely why you are sent into the world. Your family and your friends, your colleagues, and your competitors, and all the people you may meet on your journey through life are all searching for more than survival. Your presence among them as the one who is sent will allow them to catch a glimpse of the real life. (LB, p. 132)

Vespers

The quiet repetition of a single word can help us to descend with the mind into the heart. This repetition has nothing to do with magic.

It is not meant to throw a spell on God or to force him into hearing us. On the contrary, a word or sentence repeated frequently can help us to concentrate, to move to the center, to create an inner stillness and thus to listen to the voice of God. (WH, p. 81)

Compline

The mystery of God's presence therefore can be touched only by deep awareness of God's absence. It is in our longing for the absent God that we discover the footprints of the Divine One. It is in the realization of God's presence that we know that we have been touched by loving hands. It is into this mystery of divine darkness and divine light – God's absence and God's presence – that we enter when we pray. (SD, p. 80)

Salve Regina

Hail, holy Queen, Mother of mercy …

Bible Before Bed

'No one lights a lamp and puts it in some hidden place or under a tub; they put it on the lamp-stand so that people may see the light when they come in. The lamp of the body is your eye. When your eye is clear, your whole body too, is filled with light; but when it is diseased your body, too, will be darkened.' (Luke 11:33–4)

Dilexi quoniam exaudiet domin⁹: Vocem orationis mee. Quia inclinauit aurem suam michi: ⁊ in diebus meis in

WEEK FOUR

SUNDAY

Vigils

One of the discoveries we make in prayer is that the closer we come to God, the closer we come to all our brothers and sisters in the human family. God is not a private God. The god who dwells in our inner sanctuary is also the God who dwells in the inner sanctuary of each human being. (HN, p. 25)

Lauds

Detachment is often understood as letting loose of what is attractive. But it sometimes also requires letting go of what is repulsive. You can indeed become attached to dark forces such as resentment and hatred. As long as you seek retaliation, you cling to your own past. Sometimes it seems as though you might lose yourself along with your revenge and hate – so you stand there with balled-up fists, closed to the other who wants to heal you. (WHO, p. 23)

Angelus
The angel of the Lord brought tidings to Mary
And she conceived of the Holy Spirit.

Hail, Mary full of grace, the Lord is with thee:
Blessed art thou among women, and blessed is
The fruit of thy womb, Jesus. Holy Mary,
Mother of God, pray for us sinners, now and at
the hour of our death. Amen.

Behold the handmaid of the Lord:
Be it dine unto me according to your word.

Hail, Mary …

And the Word was made flesh:
And dwelt among us.

Hail, Mary …

Pray for us, O holy Mother of God:
That we may be made worthy of the promises
   of Christ.

We beseech thee, O Lord, to pour thy grace into
our hearts, that as we have known the incarnation of thy Son Jesus Christ by the message of
an angel, so by his cross and passion we may be
brought to the glory of his resurrection, through
the same Christ our Lord.

None

Jesus didn't accomplish much during his life-
time. He died as a failure. Adam didn't accomplish much either. He died as poor as he was
born. Still, both Jesus and Adam are God's
beloved sons – and they lived their sonship
among us as the only thing that they had
to offer. That is also my mission and yours.
(A, p. 37)

Vespers

Joy is essential to spiritual life. Whatever we may think or say about God, when we are not joyful, our thoughts and words cannot bear fruit. Jesus reveals to us God's love so that his joy may become ours and that our joy may become complete. (HN, p. 30)

Compline

You are confronted again and again with the choice of letting God speak or letting your wounded self cry out. Although there has to be a place where you can allow your wounded part to get the attention it needs, your vocation is to speak from the place where God dwells. (IVL, p. 99)

Salve Regina

Hail, holy Queen, Mother of mercy,
Our life, our sweetness and our hope.
To thee do we cry,
Poor banished children of Eve,

To thee do we send up our sighs,
Mourning and weeping
In this valley of tears.
Turn then, most gracious Advocate,
Thine eyes of mercy toward us,
And after this our exile,
Show unto us the blessed fruit
Of thy womb, Jesus.
O clement, O loving,
O sweet Virgin Mary!
Pray for us, O Holy Mother of God,
That we may be made worthy
Of the promises of Christ.
Amen.

Bible Before Bed

'The coming of the kingdom of God does not admit of observation and there will be no one to say "Look, it is here! Look it is there!" For look, the kingdom of God is among you.'

(Luke 17:20–1)

MONDAY

Vigils

Listening to the voice of love requires that we direct our minds and hearts toward that voice with all our attention. How can we do that? The most fruitful way – in my experience – is to take a simple prayer, a sentence or a word, and slowly repeat it. We can use the Lord's Prayer, the Jesus Prayer, the name of Jesus, or any word that reminds us of God's love and put it in the center of our inner room, like a candle in a dark space. (HN, pp. 23–4)

Lauds

Silence is full of sounds: the wind murmuring, the leaves rustling, the birds flapping their wings, the waves washing ashore. And even if these sounds cannot be heard, we still hear our own quiet breathing, the motion of our hands over our skin, the swallowing in our throats, and the soft patter of our footsteps. But we have become deaf to these sounds of silence. (WOH, p. 35)

Angelus
The Angel of the Lord brought tidings to Mary …

None
Life is a gift. Each one of us is unique, known by name, and loved by the One who fashioned us. Unfortunately, there is a very loud, consistent, and powerful message coming to us from our world that leads us to believe that we must prove our belovedness by how we look, by what we have, and by what we can accomplish … we are very slow to grasp the liberating truth of our origins and our finality. (A, p. 37)

Vespers
Joy does not simply happen to us. We have to choose joy and keep choosing it every day. It is a choice based on the knowledge that we belong to God and have found in God our refuge, and our safety and that nothing, not even death, can take God away from us. (HN, p. 31)

Compline
Everything Jesus is saying to you can be summarized in the words 'Know that you are welcome.' Jesus offers you to know all he knows and to do all he does. He wants his home to be yours. Yes, he wants to prepare a place for you in his Father's house. (IVL, p. 101)

Salve Regina
Hail, holy Queen, Mother of mercy …

Bible Before Bed
'In the same way, I tell you, there will be more

rejoicing in heaven over one sinner repenting than over ninety-nine upright people who have no need of repentance.' (Luke 15:7)

TUESDAY

Vigils

To live in the present, we must believe deeply that what is most important is the here and the now. We are constantly distracted by things that have happened in the past or that might happen in the future. It is not easy to remain focused on the present. Our mind is hard to master and keeps pulling us away from the moment. (HN, pp. 21–2)

Lauds

To be calm and quiet by yourself is not the same as sleeping. In fact, it means being fully awake and following with close attention every move going on inside of you. It requires the discipline to recognize the urge to get up and go as a temptation to look elsewhere for what is really close at hand. (WOH, p. 39)

TUESDAY

Angelus
The Angel of the Lord brought tidings to Mary …

None
The great mystery of Jesus' life is that the fulfilled his mission not in action but in passion, not by what he did but by what was done to him, not by his own decision but by other people's decisions concerning him. It was when he was dying on the cross that he cried out, 'It is fulfilled.' (A, p. 84)

Vespers
The world lies in the power of the Evil One. Indeed, the powers of darkness rule the world. We should not be surprised when we see human suffering and pain all around us. But we should be surprised by joy every time we see that God, not the Evil One, has the last word. (HN, p. 40)

[129]

Compline

Every time you can shift your attention away from the external situation that caused your pain and focus on the pain of humanity in which you participate, your suffering becomes easier to bear. It becomes a 'light burden' and an 'easy yoke' (Matthew 11:30). (IVL, p. 104)

Salve Regina

Hail, holy Queen, Mother of mercy …

Bible Before Bed

'Any kingdom which is divided against itself is heading for ruin, and house collapses against house. So, too, with Satan: if he is divided against himself, how can his kingdom last?'

(Luke 11:17–18)

WEDNESDAY

Vigils
Prayer is the discipline of the moment. When we pray, we enter into the presence of God whose name is God-with-us. To pray is to listen attentively to the One who addresses us here and now. (HN, p. 22)

Lauds
When we live from God's breath we recognize with joy that the same breath that keeps us alive is also the source of life for our brothers and sisters. This realization makes our fear of the other disappear, our weapons fall away, and brings a smile to our lips. When we recognize the breath of God in others, we can let them enter our lives and receive the gifts they offer us. (WOH, p. 55)

Angelus
The Angel of the Lord brought tidings to Mary …

Vespers
The tears of grief and the tears of joy should not be too far apart. As we befriend our pain – or, in the words of Jesus, 'take up our cross' – we discover that the resurrection is, indeed, close at hand. (HN, p. 50)

Compline
Through compassion it is possible to recognize that the craving for love that men feel resides also in our own heart, that the cruelty that the world knows all too well is also rooted in our own impulses. Through compassion we also sense our hope for forgiveness in our friends' eyes and our hatred in their bitter mouths … For a compassionate man nothing human is alien: no joy and no sorrow, no way of living and no way of dying. (WH, p. 41)

Salve Regina

Hail, holy Queen, Mother of mercy …

Bible Before Bed

'Why are you so agitated, and why are these doubts stirring in your hearts? See by my hands and my feet that it is I myself. Touch me and see for yourselves; a ghost has no flesh and bones as you can see I have.' (Luke 24:38–9)

THURSDAY

Vigils

We must learn to live each day, each hour, yes, each minute as a new beginning, as a unique opportunity to make everything new. Imagine that we could live each moment as a moment pregnant with new life. Imagine that we could live each day as a day full of promises. (HN, p. 16)

Lauds

Praying means, above all, to be accepting of God who is always new, always different. For God is a deeply moved God, whose heart is greater than our own. The open acceptance of prayer in the face of an ever-new God makes us free. (WOH, p. 58)

Angelus
The Angel of the Lord brought tidings to Mary …

Vespers
The spiritual life is the life of those who are reborn from above – who have received the Spirit of God who comes to us from God. That life allows us to break out of our prison of human entanglements and sets us free for a life in God. (HN, p. 71)

Compline
The compassionate man who points to the possibility of forgiveness helps others to free themselves from the chains of their restrictive shame, allows them to experience their own guilt, and restores their hope for a future in which the lamb and the lion can sleep together. (WH, p. 42)

Salve Regina

Hail, holy Queen, Mother of mercy …

Bible Before Bed

The next day as John stood there again with two of his disciples, Jesus went past, and John looked towards him and said, 'Look, there is the lamb of God.' And the two disciples heard what he said and followed Jesus. (John 1:35–7)

FRIDAY

Vigils

To pray is to move to the center of all life and all love. The closer I come to the hub of life, the closer I come to all that receives its strength and energy from there. My tendency is to get so distracted by the diversity of the many spokes of life, that I am busy but not truly life-giving, all over the place but not focused. By directing my attention to the heart of life, I am connected with its rich variety while remaining centered. (HN, pp. 27-8)

Lauds

In the silence of prayer you can spread out your hands to embrace nature, God, and your fellow human beings. This acceptance means not only that you are ready to look at your own limitations, but that you expect the coming of something new. For this reason, every prayer is an expression of hope. If you expect nothing from the future, you cannot pray. (WOH, p. 63)

Angelus
The Angel of the Lord brought tidings to Mary …

Vespers
Only when we claim the love of God, the love that transcends all judgments, can we overcome all fear of judgment. When we have become completely free from the need to judge others, we will also become completely free from the fear of being judged. (HN, p. 82)

Compline
For a man of prayer is, in the final analysis, the man who is able to recognize in others the face of the Messiah and make visible what was hidden, make touchable what was unreachable. (WH, p. 47)

FRIDAY

Salve Regina
Hail, holy Queen, Mother of mercy …

Bible Before Bed
'Be compassionate just as your Father is compassionate. Do not judge, and you will not be judged; do not condemn, and you will not be condemned; forgive, and you will be forgiven.'

(Luke 6:36–7)

SATURDAY

Vigils

When I pray, I enter into the depth of my own heart and find there the heart of God, who speaks to me of love. And I recognize, right there, the place where all of my sisters and brothers are in communion with one another. (HN, p. 28)

Lauds

Praying means giving up your false security, no longer looking for arguments which will protect you if you get pushed into a corner, and no longer setting your hope on a couple of lighter moments which your life might still offer. To pray means to stop expecting from God the same small-mindedness which you discover in yourself. To pray is to walk in the full light of God and to say simply, without

[140]

holding back, 'I am human and you are God.'
(WOH, p. 90)

Angelus
The Angel of the Lord brought tidings to
Mary …

Vespers
The great mystery of the spiritual life – the life
in God – is that we don't have to wait for it as
something that will happen later. Jesus says:
'Dwell in me as I dwell in you.' It is this divine
in-dwelling that is eternal life. (HN, p. 92)

Compline
For the mystic as well as for the revolutionary,
life means breaking through the veil covering
our human existence and following the vision
that has become manifest to us. Whatever we
call this vision – 'The Holy,' 'The Numinon,'
'The Spirit,' or 'Father' – we still believe that
conversion and revolution alike derive their

power from a source beyond the limitations of our own createdness. (WH, p. 20)

Salve Regina
Hail, holy Queen, Mother of mercy …

Bible Before Bed
'Whoever drinks this water
will be thirsty again;
but no one who drinks the water
that I shall give
will ever be thirsty again:
the water that I shall give
will become a spring of water within,
welling up for eternal life.'

(John 4:13–14)

Epilogue

Henri Nouwen's Theology
of the Home of Love

The house of God is a frontier region, an intense threshold where the visible world meets the ultimate but subtle structures of the invisible world. We enter this silence and stillness in order to decipher the creative depths of the divine imagination that dreams our lives. Somewhere in this kept-darkness the affection that created us waits to bless and heal us.[1]

All of us seek a home where we can feel safe and secure. And we often believe this home must be an external one. Henri Nouwen suggests in his book *Lifesigns* (entitled *Compassion* in the UK) that the New Testament offers us a theology of 'home': we find our home in Christ. Because we are baptised Christians, Nouwen says, we live in a 'house of love.' He quotes John 15:4, 'Make your home in me, as I make mine in You'[2] (Jerusalem Bible). Because Christ is our home, we are always at home no matter what occurs in or to our exterior, worldly house (life). A house can instantly disappear, as we have seen with the recent tsunami, which annihilated the houses of millions in the wink of an eye. But because we live in Christ and He in us, we are always in life and death securely and safely at home in Christ's love.

The story of the prodigal son is the parable *par excellence* of Henri Nouwen's theology of 'the home of love.' Let us revisit this parable. The son says, 'Father, give me the share of your estate that should come to me.' (Luke 15:12, New American Bible). The impatient son refuses to wait for his father's natural death; in fact, he has a 'death wish' for his father so that he can possess his inheritance now. In effect, the son is involved in psychological patricide, albeit unconsciously.

The father bestows upon his son his portion of inheritance, and the young son willingly and gladly departs to a distant country where his life degenerates into one prolonged, debauched party.

We can imagine him with his many exploitative fair-weather friends, squandering his inheritance on lust, wine and song. But soon the money vanishes and so do his friends, and he ends up alone and penniless. He hires himself out to the local citizens who offer him a job tending the swine.

What a precipitous fall for this young man: to end up working in a pigsty. To the Jewish people pigs are symbols of impurity; therefore, in his culture, his occupation is the ultimate degradation. Having abandoned his father's house of love, he now feeds pigs, better fed than he.

Hunger for food reminds him of his father's house where the hired workers have more than enough to eat. Physical hunger also reminds him of his spiritual hunger: he desperately needs to be in the presence of love and decides to return home. At first his decision to return home is the result not so much of sorrow but of pragmatism: he is poor and homeless. He also realizes that he will have to exhibit contrition when he meets his father. He prepares a brief speech, 'Father, I have sinned against heaven and against you. I no longer deserve to be called your son; treat me as you would treat one of your hired workers.' (Luke 15:18, NAB)

Is he really sorry for his actions? Has he admitted to himself his selfishness and egotism? Has he finally recognized his death wish for his father? We want to give him the benefit of the doubt and believe he is full of remorse for laying waste his life and for being unloving toward his father, but we have to admit that it looks as if he were just weary of homelessness with its concomitant loneliness and hunger.

When the father sees his son in the distance, he is filled with compassion. Eagerly the elderly father runs toward him and embraces and repeatedly kisses him. Surely he smelled the odor of pigs on his son; he likely tasted on his kissing lips the sweat, dust, and grime of his son's former life. To his astonishment, his five senses vividly proclaim the return of his lost son, a return that is nearly incredible.

We have a parable macrocosmic in scope: it can be viewed as a narrative of mankind's journey from the time of Adam to now or we can see it as a microcosmic story of a young man, now a full member of the family of man, one who reeks of sin. The father's vision, however, penetrates beyond the filthy clothes, the odorous smells and degradation, all of which symbolize his son's sinful life. The eye of love sees through the surface to his son's true self, and he immediately orders his servants to, 'Quickly bring the finest robe and put it on him; put a ring on his finger and sandals on his feet.' (Luke 15:22, NAB)

We have now before us an instant make-over. The external man is bathed, perfumed, dressed, sandaled and finally jeweled. The agapetic father reminds his son of his beloved sonship. The father is not involved in a restoration of the status of sonship, for in his mind and heart his son was never anything but his son; therefore, restoration is unnecessary.

We understand from a human standpoint that his father could have said 'I told you so.' He could have said, 'Out of my sight! You are no longer worthy to be called my son.' He could have said, like King Lear in literature's most powerful rejection of a child,

Here I disclaim all my paternal care,
Propinquity, and property of blood,
And as a stranger to my heart and me
Hold thee from this forever.

(*King Lear*, Act I, sc. 1)

Instead, the father orders what rightfully belongs to his son by having his servants dress him in the 'finest robe.' Another translation says the 'best robe,' but the Greek actually means the 'first robe.' Metropolitan Anthony suggests that one doesn't wear the best (or finest) robe to be comfortable at home. He likely meant for his servants to retrieve the robe that his son had worn on the day he left, the one his son quickly tore off and carelessly discarded, the robe his father lovingly picked up, folded and put away as Isaac had done with his son Joseph's many-coloured robe spattered with the blood of his seeming death.[3]

The father also gives his son a ring, which is not an ordinary ring. When people could not write, the ring was used as a seal to guarantee documents. To give one's ring to someone meant that you were placing your life into his hands.

The father demands nothing of his son; he wants only to have him back home where he can express his love for him, where he can relish his presence. And as in all cultures, the way to let people know you love and appreciate them is to throw a party. The father gleefully shouts out the order, 'Take the fattened calf and slaughter it. Then let us celebrate with a feast, because this son of mine was dead, and has come to life again, he was lost and has been found.' (Luke 15:24, NAB)

The father's tacit plea, expressed in his commands to his servants is, 'Let me love and treasure you because you are my beloved son. Let me celebrate your return. Let me proclaim to our world your value to me: you are more valuable than all my property, far beyond the worldly value of clothes, rings, and livestock.'

The father is, of course, offering his son a new life, a new innocence, a new start. The slate has been wiped clean. And because of the nature of Agape – unconditional love – even if the son again falters and fails, he will be forgiven over and over again. About forgiveness, Philip Toynbee says,

God's forgiveness is not an action, or even an activity, but a permanent condition. To know that my sin is forgiven at the very moment of its being committed is the true state of penitence.[4]

In this parable, Christ shows us how a father sees his children. Indeed, Christ need not imagine how a father acts; he knows the Being of his Father, 'I and the Father are One.' Christ offers us a glimpse of how God the Father loves, but at the same time, it also illustrates how Christ loves those who are lost, alienated and wandering in a distant country of sin. We can imagine Christ saying, 'Come home! Drop what you are doing, forget your sins and speed your way back home, for there is no need for you ever to be homeless. Return to your home of love prepared for you from the beginning of time.'

Let us go more deeply.

In Robert Frost's narrative poem 'The Death of the Hired Man', the character Warren says: 'Home is the place where/ when you have to go there,/ They have to take you in.' His wife Mary responds, 'I should have called it/ Something you somehow haven't to deserve.'

What do we deserve? Joan Chittister says,

> We didn't earn God. We didn't ever deserve God. We couldn't possibly deserve God. We only had to be conscious of God and grow into the life force that already lived in us.[5]

Therefore, as Christians, deserving is never a consideration. We do not have to deserve forgiveness or love because we are eternally welcomed here and now: Jesus is always within, his arms outstretched to greet and to embrace us: we are invited to the Feast no matter what we have done or not done with our lives.

Let us look at the son's contrition. When the son initially thinks that he would be better off at home where he would be better fed, he composes his first act of contrition, an imperfect one because his impulse is a selfish one: he is homeless, hungry and friendless. But on the journey home he had time for an examination of conscience.

Alone and quiet, the son soon sees his imperfect sorrow transform into perfect contrition: he is truly sorry for wasting his inheritance because he had carelessly tossed away love, just as he had mindlessly tossed away his first robe and later the pods to the pigs he fed. However, rejecting love is not love's disappearance: It remains present and available to us at all times. All we need do is turn ourselves toward it (*metanoia*). We do not have to move, for like the father, Love (God is the Prime Mover) instantly rushes toward us, for Love bears all things, hopes all things, and endures all things. Although we may falter and fail again and again, Love never fails, and we are never separated from it. St. Paul reminds us,

> For I am convinced that neither death, nor life, nor angels, nor principalities, nor present things, nor future things, nor powers, nor height, nor depth, nor any other creature will be able to separate us from the love of God in Christ Jesus our Lord. (Romans 8:35, NAB)

How fortunate we are to live not in a fragile glass house but in a home that will endure forever: our Home of Love.

Coda When I had finished the above essay, which I had prepared for a Henri Nouwen Retreat at Glastonbury Abbey in Hingham, Massachusetts, I sent it off as an e-mail attachment to my friend Professor Richard Whitfield for his commentary. At the very time I sent my e-mail, Richard had been reading a favorite author and came across this passage,

> The climate of God's love for us in Christ means that we are never put down but always lifted up; never put out into the cold, but always brought into the warmth … The prodigal son was not asked to change his clothes in the pigsty among people who despised him. This was asked of him when he was already home, in the warm acceptance of his father's never interrupted acceptance and care. His transformation would begin, so to speak, with a bath in front of the kitchen fire. As the old rags that smelt of pigs were being thrown to the back of the fire, the new clothes are already hanging over a chair, aired and warm. His father is there, delighting in

his son, half the grown man he is, half the child he used to be and needs to be again. The servants all reflect the father's unconditional positive regard ... The door is shut on the cold draught of the elder brother's criticism. This is the climate that most of us need if a total down-to-the-skin change of inner and outer personality clothing is to take place.

You don't know how cold you are until you come into the warmth, how anxious you are until you come into peace. This peace passes all understanding, because it isn't the least bit threatened or diminished by your giving way for the pent-up anxiety to express itself fully. It welcomes you as you are. This is the Gospel![6]

Needless to say, I was delighted with this wise and insightful exegesis of the return of the prodigal son, so much so that I feel compelled to include it in what I first considered a finished meditation.

Is it finished now? No, it is not completed, for now is the time for you to return to the good news of the Gospel and read for yourself Christ's parable of the home of love.

Endnotes

1. John O'Donohue *Beauty, The Invisible Embrace* (San Francisco: HarperCollins, 2004), p. 160.
2. Henri Nouwen, *Lifesigns* (New York: Doubleday & Co., 1986), p. 37.
3. Anthony Bloom (Metropolitan Anthony), *Meditations on a Theme* (New York: Continuum, 1972), pp. 73–88.
4. Philip Toynbee, *Part of a Journey, An Autobiographical Journal 1977–1979* (London: Collins, 1981), p. 337.
5. Joan Chittister, *Called to Question* (New York: Sheed and Ward, 2004), p. 40.
6. Frank Lake, *The Spirit of Truth*, ed. Carol Christian, pp. 94–95.

Bibliography

Week One

The Wounded Healer (New York: Doubleday, 1979; London: Darton, Longman and Todd, new edition, 1994)

The Inner Voice of Love (New York: Doubleday, 1998; London: Darton, Longman and Todd, 1997)

Making All Things New (New York: Harper & Row, 1981)

The Return of the Prodigal Son (New York: Doubleday, 1994; London: Darton, Longman and Todd, 1994)

Lifesigns, (New York: Doubleday: 1986; London: Darton, Longman and Todd, 2008, new edition, published in the UK as *Compassion*)

The Genesee Diary (New York: Doubleday, 1981; London: Darton, Longman and Todd, new edition, 1995)

With Burning Hearts (Maryknoll: Orbis Books, 1994)

Clowning in Rome (New York: Doubleday, 1979)

Week Two

Reaching Out (New York: Doubleday: 1975)

Can You Drink the Cup? (Notre Dame: Ave Maria Press, 1996). Copyright © 1972, 1995, 2005 by Ave Maria Press, P.O. Box 428, Notre Dame, IN 46556, www.avemariapress.com

Sabbatical Journey (New York: Crossroad Publishing Company, 1998; London: Darton, Longman and Todd, 1998)

Spiritual Journals (New York: Continuum Publishing, 1998)

[158]

Week Three

Life of the Beloved (New York: Crossroad Publishing Company, 1992; London: Hodder & Stoughton, 1993)

The Way of the Heart (San Francisco: HarperCollins Publishers, 1981; London: Darton, Longman and Todd, third edition, 1999)

The Selfless Way of Christ (Maryknoll: Orbis, 2007; London: Darton, Longman and Todd, 0000)

Intimacy (New York: HarperCollins Publishers, 1969)

Spiritual Direction (San Francisco: HarperSanFrancisco, 2006)

Week Four

With Open Hands (Notre Dame: Ave Maria Press, 1972). Copyright © 1996 by Ave Maria Press, P.O. Box 428, Notre Dame, IN 46556, www.avemariapress.com

Here and Now (New York: Crossroad Publishing, 1994; London: Darton, Longman and Todd, 1994)

Adam (Maryknoll: Orbis, 1997; London: Darton, Longman and Todd, 1997)

The Wounded Healer (New York: Doubleday, 1979; London: Darton, Longman and Todd, new edition, 1994)

The Inner Voice of Love (New York: Doubleday, 1998; London: Darton, Longman and Todd, 1997)

Illustrations

p.2: Ms 63 f.73r The Flight from Bethlehem, from a Book of Hours, *c.*1460 (vellum) by French School, (15th century). Fitzwilliam Museum, University of Cambridge, UK/ The Bridgeman Art Library

ILLUSTRATIONS

p.7: 1488.5; Adoration of the Trinity, from a Book of Hours printed by Philippe Pigouchet for Simon Vostre, 1498 (vellum) by French School, (15th century). © Lambeth Palace Library, London, UK/ The Bridgeman Art Library

p.17: Additional 18855: Boating in the month of May, from a Book of Hours, c.1540 (vellum) by Bening, Simon (c.1483–1561). Victoria & Albert Museum, London, UK/ The Bridgeman Art Library

p. 53: Add 18855 October: ploughing and sowing, from a Book of Hours, c.1540 (vellum) by Bening, Simon (c.1483–1561).Victoria & Albert Museum, London, UK/ The Bridgeman Art Library.

p.87: Add 18855 April: courting couples, from a Book of Hours, c.1540 (vellum) by Bening, Simon (c.1483–1561). Victoria & Albert Museum, London, UK/ The Bridgeman Art Library.

p. 117: 1488.5 Dives and Lazarus, from a Book of Hours printed by Philippe Pigouchet for Simon Vostre, 1498 (vellum) by French School, (15th century). © Lambeth Palace Library, London, UK/ The Bridgeman Art Library.

p. 143: Ms Lat. Q.v.I.126 f.53 David defending his father's sheep against a lion, from the 'Book of Hours of Louis d'Orleans'. 1469 (vellum). Colombe, Jean (c.1430–c.93)/ National Library, St. Petersburg.